First Fleet

First Fleet

Michael Crowley

STACK
BOOKS

Smokestack Books
1 Lake Terrace, Grewelthorpe, Ripon HG4 3BU
e-mail: info@smokestack-books.co.uk
www.smokestack-books.co.uk

ISBN 978-0-9934547-2-1

Smokestack Books is represented by Inpress Ltd

For Rosa

We see things not as they are, but as we are.
The Talmud

Contents

Time Signature

Foreword

In May 1787 eleven ships left Portsmouth bound for Botany Bay on the south eastern coast of what was then called New Holland. Their cargo was eight hundred convicts and a year's worth of supplies. They had little knowledge of the land they were attempting to settle or its inhabitants. The ambitious endeavour of the First Fleet was led by Captain Arthur Phillip with around two hundred marines under his command. That all eleven ships got there at all, and all within days of each other, is remarkable. An extraordinary feat of seamanship and navigation. A journey of fifteen thousand miles through stretches of under-explored ocean in eight months and one week. The experience of the ships' crews is an epic story in itself.

For the first few years the existence of the settlement was precarious. The thousand or so new inhabitants were faced with crop failure, drought, diminishing rations in a strange and uncharted land where the seasons were in reverse. They had little to go on to begin with. Cook's charts were sketchy and the reports of his naturalist Joseph Banks erroneous in some respects. Of course the British had the experience of colonisation elsewhere, yet this had limited currency with the people with whom they struggled to build relations.

The events have come to us through eleven journals and letters, mainly by the marine officers. There are no convict journals and there are no records from Aboriginal people. Though plainly told, the journals are extraordinary reading for they concern, often rather casually, events of great historical significance. They remind us how our present was once balanced on the edge of individual endeavour. The very survival of the settlement at Sydney Cove depended upon the rescue mission of the *Sirius* circumnavigating the globe at below forty degrees to purchase supplies from Cape Hope; to a lesser degree the efforts of convict farmer James Ruse. Events that are terrible and fascinating: the execution of Thomas Barret; Arthur Phillip's relationship with Bennelong. Necessarily they are viewed through the screen of a colonisation that led to a disaster for the

Aboriginal people, its opening chapter the smallpox epidemic in the spring of 1789.

What is absent from many primary sources are the private, intimate voices we long to hear; those of the marines, of the convicts and Aboriginal people. These I have occupied with poetry. Both people about whom there is memoir and biography as well as those about whom we only know name and sentence. What follows will not add to the history of the First Fleet. I would dearly love to do that but poetry can't help. The sequence was borne from an impossible desire to enter history, to get closer to the dead and the silent to whom we are indebted, whether we know it or whether we like it, or not.

Michael Crowley

First Fleet

Condemned

Susannah Ruse, Bodmin Assizes, 29 July 1782

James in the dock, handsome, filthy from gaol.
Caught in the silversmith's house at night,
two watches in his pocket, cheese in his mouth.
In front of a judge now, chin stuck out.

Married me in Lawhitton,
Lizzie already twisting in my belly.
She's a prowling cat. Hasty James,
has an ocean of fields to teal now.

I'll not roar like others in the gallery. He,
no sadder than our wedding night, his lips write,
Wait for me. The pushed aside, eldest son is hanged,
reprieved, transported seven years.

Gawky James, farmhand
with a farmer's family to feed, I said
the silversmith would have a pistol.
One watch would have done wouldn't it?

James Ruse, face like Growan clay,
will pull a plough in his burgling clothes,
labouring right through our nights
as he crosses off his days.

Chimney Sweep

John Hudson on the prison hulk Dunkirk, the Thames 1785

My character has been marked down as very good.
Sometimes I cannot help and I am troublesome.

If I am marked down good again, I could be moved up deck.
James Grace will sink lower if he carries on.

He swills rum like a tinker, tells me it tastes like rag water.
He has tongue enough for two sets of teeth and pretends he is a man,

but I know he lies down with a molly for half his ration.
I have my chain off now and am too fast for them.

They have brought on women, given 'em the top deck.
They whine and cry and fight - rum vixens off their hooks.

The overseer says we'll sail to Bot'ny Bay New Wales
and there work onshore all day. I am finished with chimneys

the soot and the sores, and too big besides.
I would gladly make shoes if a master would show me.

James says we will be pardoned because of our age.
He can't be believed. He is a codshead, bad at sneaks and cracks,

was caught three times by Runners. We have no fever on our deck
they have it below us. I will ask to be chained to another boy.

Charlotte Medal

Thomas Barrett on board the Charlotte, October 1787

A catch poll nabbed my father.
A maker of tools and crippled bob pieces
he learned me a fob is best done on the sly.

I struck out on my own still young,
working sneaks on Clerkenwell Road,
up to High Holborn; as servants brushed steps

I gutted houses, drew the King's picture,
was plump in the pocket
till the day came for my own morning drop.

Sent instead on a lag-ship for America,
we convicts mutinied, made easy the crew.
Yet I missed my dance again, now for Botany Bay.

The surgeon summons me to his cabin,
bids me engrave an image of the *Charlotte*,
on his silver kidney dish,

I draw for rations and kindness,
for my own quiet, for I have run out of dice.
I draw a ship, anchored at night.

Diplomacy

Governor designate Arthur Phillip lands at Botany Bay,
18 January 1788

The coast of New South Wales sighted – a dream in heavy seas
emerging then receding – morning, January third.

Seven thousand miles of ocean in fifty one days,
then a fortnight in the vice of easterlies, southerlies,

holding us all the last leagues to Botany Bay.
January eighteen, late afternoon. An open boat to the shore,

Ruse, a Cornish convict, carries Lieutenant Dawes
on his back to the beach, sets him down.

Beyond the sands: marsh and swamp, trees half submerged,
not the heathland and meadows Cook mentions at all.

Some distance up the strand, a party of natives
have emerged armed with lances taller than a man.

They are without clothing, some wear white paint.
One after another they cry, *Waroo, waroo.*

I approach, tell them my name, pull from my pocket
an eye-glass, red baize, bright beads, place them on the ground.

One lays his lance down, takes up the beads, another the baize,
I tie some around his arm, stand amongst them.

They are tranquil, unoffending. I point to my ship
in the distance show them through the eye glass.

They repeat *Waroo waroo* and leave.
I place some beads in the stern of their canoe.

Badlands

Jane Fitzgerald, Sydney Cove, February 1788

Just the shine off them, the blackberries of home.
Bread dipped in butter, and chestnuts and eels.
My mouth is sore from fancying.

But I am not at sea now. I have my rations
without the pleasure of marines. They are ill-tempered.
Vermin won't leave them be.

One who knew me on the *Charlotte*
struck another for two words to me.
He's to be lashed for that. Won't know his coat from his back.

After that I will go into the woods
lie all night in the dews with a highway robber.
A mutinous man.

We make free out here, of the land and the sea,
of each other. Marriage means nothing.
Seven or eight die each day.

There is talk of taking men to some island
weeks east. So red and rocky the earth
so fevered men behave.

They watch the lightning off the bay,
or look behind the camp up-river,
to China they say.

First up the Fig Tree

Surgeon White at the execution of Thomas Barrett, February 1788

Fruit bats twitch in the fig tree,
the sun about to set. Muck drips
from a row of black caps.

We are all here. All except his Excellency,
Nicholls beside the ladders.
He didn't need much convincing.

The chaplain leads them in.
Lovell, Hall and the boy Barrett,
born on Newgate's steps.

They eye the crowd, Lovell smiles.
The Reverend can scarcely walk.
Surly boots is about to retch,

just like the day they unloaded the women.
The men winding up the clock all night,
marines first then convicts, drunk as Davy's sows.

They are taken to the fatal tree,
their nooses tied. They stole property
of the Crown: beef and pease.

Barrett, a convict of guile and craft,
coined quarter dollars out of buckles,
pewter spoons, on the passage from Santa Cruz.

I had him brought to my cabin,
gave the boy a dish of plated silver.
He fashioned a medallion in the dimness of the hold.

A message from the Governor's house.
Lovell and Hall are reprieved. Now the Reverend
is alone with Barrett's eyes.

Faith drips off his face, soaks his Bible.
The boy confesses, *I've led a very wicked life,*
knows his death is deserved.

He is hardy at the end. Nicholls pulls the ladder,
a rag shakes in the wind. A river in the sky,
squealing clods of bats head out to feed.

Reflections on a Recent Expedition

Arthur Phillip, First Governor of New South Wales,
about his ablutions, March 1788

Eight miles northward to Cook's broken land.
Captain Tench with convicts in a longboat, the cutter under my
    command.
Against the ebb tide all day, much slowed about the headland.

Whirlwinds and rain, pelicans in great number
then among the bluest stretch of water I have seen,
the land much higher here, within reach only to birds, covered in
    timber.

Natives upon the rocks, arms like raised oars.
We are bobbing about like fools on a rope's end when
an old man points to a channel, a youth motions us in from the shore.

The old man fetches us fire, behind him the women,
one sings a song much to our liking.
All their left hand little fingers have two joints missing.

The men are scarred, wind blows beneath their skin.
They conduct us to a cave. Faces painted with pipe clay,
walls with red ochre. Tench beckons me withdraw.

The old man is offended. Two teeth missing from his left jaw,
his beard singed at its end. He helps us build
a canopy of ferns between our boats on the shore.

I present him with gifts - nails, beads, a red kersey jacket to wear.
He dances for some time then steals a cutlass, I hold him,
slap him about his shoulders. He brandishes his spear,

my men are about their musketry, the old man vents his rage.
He is brave, they are all this way. But they will not come to camp.
Our ragged settlement.This hungry, ashen, tent.

The bush-rat comes every night, and beetles like dice
with their dogs' appetite. The quartermaster he comes,
with news of more thefts from the supplies.

Tench comes to say the carpenters are sick,
Ruse, he comes, to say rank grass has killed the cattle,
that the gum tree, *Not unlike our willow in leaf*, always splits,

sinks in the water. But they do not come -
the men with their shell-tipped lances, in bark canoes,
their language abounding with vowels.

Nor the old man, the smell of fish oil off him.
He wants nothing from us. Refuses my table,
they will not come here to our aid. His beard is burned away.

Making Mortar

Jane Fitzgerald, Rushcutters Bay, April 1788

All day I pick up oyster shells.
Nothing divides us from the sun,
no wind or cloud, or shade.
There are no pearls,
just the pummelled milk white ears
listening to their own rattle in our sacks.

We drag them through the trees,
under shrilling birds to the clay-field.
Men are folded to the ground,
stooped like horses nibbling the earth.

Bloodworth gives the orders.
He stands straight, chest out,
works men hard to have brick houses built.
The Governor imagines a town,
fine houses like Bristol.
Rations are down, still Bloodworth will kill
to have his Highness's house made.

He told a soldier to shoot a native woman
throwing stones at labourers from a tree.
I screamed – the soldier looked at me,
then she jumped and was gone.
A shell is also a blade.

Learning the Language: I

Governor Arthur Phillip orders the barber to the beach, May 1788

They come out of the woods to the barber's chair.
A group of four. One wears bones in his hair, the teeth

of dogs, lobster claws. The ship's barber laughs with them,
beards falling to his feet, he holds up a mirror

passed from hand to hand. Dawes takes off his jacket,
puts it on the shoulders of a squat man,

two teeth missing from the front of his mouth.
He says a word in their unutterable language:

Goorobeera he cries, finger on a musket.
Dawes makes the shape with his lips.

Each in turn voice the word, newly born
it moves back and forth. Dawes points to his nose,

his ear, summoning a language. Waves lap
close to the chair. They retreat seizing the jacket.

The barber bids them back, they shout *Wo-roo-wo-roo*
pointing to the sea. Dawes heads for his tent, his dictionary

of native speech. They argue from the trees.
The tide comes for their hair, singed ringlets hang in the breeze.

Damned

James Daley fears for survival, June 1788

We have the rations of the hanged, the otherwise dead.
When the stores have bled out
we will have to face natives in the woods.

Ruse's farm can't feed bats.
They watch from trees stripped bare more half asleep than us,
move off quietly for food somewhere.

The Governor talks of a city. He has drawings under his bed.
Lies stricken with sickness, a landed fish in another world.
He won't keep Christmas here.

Only one ship left in the bay.
The *Sirius* gone for grain to bring back flour for bones.
I'd say the crew will whip ashore, hide in the port.

Poor Barrett turned off up the ladder,
tail flapping for a handful of pork.
A storm the same day washed him out his grave.

There is gold somewhere here. Why else would we have come?
The livestock have walked off inland.
I might take that ship. Join with others become a whaling man.

Crop Failure

James Ruse to Governor Arthur Phillip, July 1788

Sir, nature dislikes us here.
Six months louster on eight acres
grubbing up roots, hacking at gums, felling trees
twenty five feet about the trunk.
No plough or beasts, all hack and peck hoe.

Men break and die. One I know a lead miner,
laid down arms folded on his breast,
the yellow ground his tomb. I shut his eyes for him.

Barley and corn eaten by weevils, mice,
all else that moves after dark.
This is a land of night, it does not want a farm.
The sky won't allow it.

Famished soil, mean as Cornish clay,
washes off the rock, air thick with lightning.
Natives throw spears behind trees
yet you send to England to bring them clothes.
Nature has come too far.

I was bred a farmer, others laboured at purses,
their minds are afeard of work. They gaze up at birds
dreaming of English Aprils and September apples.
They have worked and died only for more seed.
They have tasted this earth and spit out my name with it.

I carried your lieutenant to the shore, my feet first on the ground,
my arms the first to hoe. In a year my time is done.
Bid me the first to go home.

Sermon

Reverend Richard Johnson, chaplain to the Colonies, July 1788

Where lies the bounty of this land? Not in
the ground, its trees, the windless firmament
chaining us to the shade. Man must dig in,
crowbar the roots, break his instruments

ploughing, praying to seasons in reverse.
We shall perish with the crop or the harvest,
become the juice that sweetens the earth
without the witness of a church, only the marvel

of the gospels in my hand. At some services
natives stand amongst the convicts, they seem
to understand in the measure of the silences
we bring a clean thing out of the unclean.
An eagle above us bathes in the spa of the air.
His vexed eye hunts for game that isn't there.

Flogging Duty

Surgeon White oversees the punishment of James Daley,
August 1788

Flesh hardened, skull thickened, eyes deepened,
led again to the triangle or the tree.
The drummer boy's roll, a sentence mumbled,
black strap in the mouth, whip shook out,
hands tied high, heels off the ground,
skin pulled tight. Not much of a crowd.
A ludicrous man, claimed he'd found a goldmine.
Hundred lashes this time, shoulder to buttock

the cat collects his flesh, throws it back in our faces.
Pieces loop over heads like sea spray, thinning
in the wind. Cockroaches carry portions away.
Barangaroo the native woman, wails from the woods,
runs about naked, waves a branch at the major.
The bone's exposed. White as cockatoo feathers.
Bathe with salt water, cover the mess with leaves.
This is what a New Holland surgeon does with his day.

This is what a New Holland surgeon does with his day.
Bathe with salt water, cover the mess with leaves.
Barangaroo naked, shoulder to buttock.
Not much of a crowd. To the triangle or the tree,
black strap in the mouth, hands tied, heels off the ground,
skin pulled tight. Wails from the woods.
Flesh hardened, skull thickened, eyes deepened.
A ludicrous man, thinning in the wind.

Illustrating a Journal

Surgeon White paints the crested cockatoo, September 1788

The gamekeeper brings me birds he has slain,
a kingfisher without its head to match.
I sought out its colours up-river and found
a crest that glows gaily against its back,

like the silver darlings that shone about
our ships all the days of the doldrums,
until with the grampus we drifted south
carried by the spawn of the ocean.

Scurvy taints the convicts' skin sallow white.
Faces are clouds, mouths are parrot tails;
a runaway was found blackened by lightning.
The sky is bruised, it will bring more hail.
My cockatoo prances along the chair,
his black eyes in the mirror keep him there.

Mercy

Seaman Jacob Nagle on board the Sirius, October 1788

Seamen are not convicts.
The way the continent has it
positons are ice islands, ebbing, slipping.

Convict, marine, Governor, seaman
are false landfalls
crawled upon, starved, whipped.

A native sits at the Governor's table
while we are taken with scurvy
scudding the Horn in search of supplies.

Behind us every ghost lives a week
on five pounds of flour, four of pork
two pints of pease.

Whales are about us soaking the deck.
In the watch we have but thirteen left,
that with the carpenter's crew.

Tied below the third lieutenant screams
*Tip all nines and we'll see
if she rises for a set of damned rascals.*

We saw land but three miles off.
The captain brought his charts on deck.
He overhauled them. We saw surf,

trees, hills there were, brush and woods.
A man died in sight of it.
Then it vanished. The Cape Flyaway.

I have my ring, my buckles.
If we reach Table Bay I'll trade my seamanship,
return no more to Sydney Cove.

A Convict Can Sail

Samuel Bird on the prospects of escape, January 1789

I was chained to William Bryant on the hulk.
Our two feet in step, our legs in a dance on deck,
picking lice off our backs. We walked and slept as one.

I watched the flesh flicked off his shoulders by the cat,
his sides turned to jelly and he did not weep.
A hundred lashes then he walks over to his wife

standing straighter than in our hulk days.
This man can navigate. Stars are like words to him.
He can catch a handful of wind, tickle currents like salmon,

read rain in the birds. Only one ship left in the bay,
the *Sirius* gone to the Cape for food.
We have a compass, a tomahawk tucked away.

Bennelong the black is with us.
We will take the cutter, six oars and a mast,
glide into the cove, shadow the north points of the bay.

Healing

Jane Fitzgerald receives twenty five lashes for disobedience, March 1789

I only talked with William. We like to talk with each other;
our corner in the shade. But Bloodworth the brick-master,
the henhouse sneak, has folk flogged now, easy as a major.

William went to plead but mister Tench said
I have written the sentence down. William said,
Count every second stroke Jane.

I couldn't count after five. I pressed my face
into the tree like it was my mother's skirts,
Bloodworth shouting *Damned bitch* from the crowd.

I saw my daughters in Bristol.
The girls taller, waist high to their father at the gate.
Their faces clean, hair shining, their mouths shut bravely tight.
When it stops my eldest holds my hand. We walk to my hut.

Women are separate from the men now.
We have our own fires and places.
But William, he nurses me.
His narrow fingers, soft as water make me sleep.
I dread the flies that's all. Footsteps along my wounds,
the shiver of their eggs.

William is no soldier. His uniform hangs off his shoulders,
he is young, taunted and ordered by all others.
But he brings me the healing leaves,
sets down his musket, reaches for me.
I will sew his torn sleeves.

Landed

Arabanoo of the Gayimai People fails to escape captivity,
March 1789

The English caught me in their net,
mister Tench he laughs at me.
I was a dolphin with nowhere to dive to,
held afloat by a skin of clothes,
so they pulled me from the sea

bound me about at my arms and neck.
Their women came to look at me
as he led me through the camp
butterfly children about my feet,
where is mister Tench taking me?

My people lie under crabs
faces like pitted stones,
they crawl to camp for fish and fire,
cry when the English whip their own.
Their throats dry their skin foams.

They ask about living with white men,
their eyes are always the same,
I close them, bury or burn them
at a place where the captain says.
They are lizards in the flames.

Warrane is a land of the dead.
It has come ashore and will not go away.
Where is mister Tench taking me
in this house that floats out
towards the jaws of the bay?

Learning the Language: II

Surgeon White on the smallpox epidemic, April 1789

The woods are aflame. The land burns black.
We leave prints in ash, deeper and deeper
west from the cove. All the country catches
fire, burnt by natives, by us and even

of its own accord. Trees become chimneys.
Now a gale of smallpox blows. Boat crews
report natives dead, left without ceremony
at cave entrances and beaches, a few

we find sit alone by burning sticks,
eyes blank and sunken. A boy pours water
from a shell onto his father's lips
broken by sores. He stands, points at the old man
his eyes on me. *Bo-ee… bo-ee,* he cries.
A word for death. He is called Nanbaree.

Galgalla

Surgeon White on the death of Arabanoo through smallpox,
April 1789

We have brought our blood here and it sickens.
Centuries of malady flows within us.
A plague once asleep now stirs and quickens,
hunts among the natives laying blisters

and lesions, they come to us with slow muscles.
I have measured in my mind's eye the size
of the fluid held in perfect pustules
carried by a small boy alone. It thrives

the pox in foaming quarts. Tench tramps
for days, it greets him across wide rivers,
Arabanoo who nursed the sick, perished.
There is malady in the gifts we give,
in what we say, sickness in what we take.
He was blithe and brave, poisoned by a snake.

Discovery

Captain Tench explores west of Rose Hill, June 1789

We march in fearful silence steering west
by north following the vee of geese
to other waterfowl. Before us stretches
an untamed abyss, unknown to European

feet. A crow caws over its kingdom,
spins to the grass with a single shot.
There are signs of Indians at every mile,
bird and squirrel traps, bark hunting huts

like two playing cards folded in the middle.
We make camp at a pond and broil the crow.
Next noon we turn back faced with a river
yet to be named. Indians come, they labour
with pox. I think on the Thames at Putney.
Ducks hear gunfire for the first time and flee.

Desecration

Bennelong of the Eora People is taken prisoner, November 1789

They feed me well. I wear their clothes,
their rope around my ankles.
Woolawarre is a friend with power.
There are sounds that cannot be made
in each other's mouths, visions
that cannot be shared, we are
as different times of the same day.

They will not honour Kayoo-May.
I have said to Woolawarre,
You cut down trees and fish without asking.
They have sunk canoes, hunted the kangaroo.
They are a lost people, fallen from the wrong sky
to make a disease. Days and days
of ceremony for the dead,

I am too tired to weep.
My dream said they would never leave.
They have weapons I can steal,
hatchets to fight the Cameraigal.
I will eat more turtle, drink the strong drink,
cut my rope and run to the trees,
back to my wife, Barangaroo.

The World Dried

Jane Fitzgerald on the death of her infant son James,
January 1790

One night in his life it rained.
I stood out in it, held him up,
each drop a bucketful on his head.

He awoke, looked at me, made a sound.
The rain brought down a coolness.
My son seemed to speak of its loveliness.

Then heat fell like never before,
a furnace and a swarm. My milk dried.
The chaplain brought over grapes,

I rubbed the juice on James's lips.
A pip trembled there,
I wiped it away and he sucked my finger.

The chaplain laid him near his house,
he says a church will be built by the graveyard.
It was he who made the cross, not his father.

His name is carved and the weeks.
I have his smell on me, made stronger by the sun,
his sound still in this hut.

Home

James Ruse to Susannah Ruse, Rose Hill, February 1790

Susannah, have you expected to see me
walking through Launceston on market day?
Maybe. Doubt you been counting the time.
If Lizzie has survived then she will be nine.
Perhaps she is next to you now, counting swallows in a line.
There are swallows here but coloured like a robin.
They leave when yours arrive.

I can read the year now. Planting and reaping is at odds
with England but I have it right.
I am the farmer here, chosen by the Governor.
A man that would know His Majesty
cleared me some acres, built me a hut,
watches my progress towards his promise of a farm.

Nine rods a day, I hoed it all up,
dug in the timber ashes, let it lie under the sun.
Sowed three bushels of seed on my wheat land
not like the Cove farm, this time properly done.
I gained my freedom a year ago, yet I will wait.
See what the weather holds.

I miss the cold, the look of frost and snow.
The sleep it brings. I am by a river, it can
give off a gold sheen on hot days. In May
it sweats a fog and you could be in Cornwall.
You would like the land. But not the company
or the conversation. Work is my only master
and the fields don't have an end.

Plenty

Jane Fitzgerald on Norfolk Island, March 1790

Each day we take the birds and their eggs.
Pull them from their holes or else dig them out
as they cry in our hands.

They fly down in their thousands everywhere on the island,
there isn't room in the sky. They are pushed up high
as they come ashore like boats on the tide,

drop onto trees, even the ground at our feet.
Some are stupid tame with us,
I threw one up to fly but it came back to be my meat.

We snatch them by their bellies, plump in our hands.
Hudson the chimney sweep boy
fits his wrist into any crevice, tears out the bird,

turns its neck like the handle on a door,
puts it down his breeches. I've seen him
drink their blood, eat the eggs raw.

He said to me, *I have plenty fat ones buried under stones.*
The air is thick with feathers, the souls of birds.
We will eat them for as long as they come.

Proposal

James Hudson to Jane Fitzgerald, April 1790

If we kiss again we should go and see the major.
Even if we sit close we might be flogged
if reported by a soldier.
So Jane, I say we should speak of our feelings
or else we swallow them whole.

When I was a sweep, come May
after the last fires were lit,
we were left alone till winter.
Only boys working together ate through the summer.
Like the way we bag the birds here, in pairs.

No one cries for her that jumped from the cliffs today.
She couldn't bear the island, gave in to the ocean.
She was alone. I find this no harder
than my life in London. My mind is grown,
I have spirit to give away.

I see through you to the bottom of the well.
When we walk in the woods, amongst trees like castles,
our loneliness leaves in the quiet.
Just the wind on our clothes,
a scream from the ghost of a bird.

Second Fleet

Norfolk Island, August 1790

I am Catherine Crowley, taken to Norfolk Island.
I have this day born a son. His left eye waters,
is turned in. Otherwise he is sturdy.

His father pulled him towards the bloodstained light.
A gentleman felon, a chancer who claims
his line from Ireland's earls. Darcy.

I come from peasants and rogues, they wait
in ditches, on roads for the gallows or the voyage,
still it was me that Darcy chose on the lag-ship.

The ground rolls under our feet, we shamble
like geese with the bracelets. Our son though
will grow his land-legs, rise like an earl.

The Major is lappy with the lash. Whipped even
the flogging man for laying on easy. They have Darcy
as a surgeon, standing by the stake when wretches faint.

Marines ripen by the day, Darcy hears talk of a rising,
swaggers about the shire on broken shells,
brings me mutton-birds and eggs.

Prayer

Reverend Richard Johnson, Sydney Cove, August 1790

We are a wicked people, truly. Blind
to the commands of government and God.
I watch men think on the end of their time
who would trade their souls for a cup of grog.

Judgement has made us prisoners of a drought,
now twice forty days. Birds fall from trees expired,
the soil is nought, night no respite, water
scarce. Couples lie down in huts to die.

How oft shall my brother sin against me?
I have taken in a native, taught her the Lord's
Prayer, taken great pains with acres, feed us
they shall if you send gracious rain as reward.
My duty is to abide where I am,
acquire four hundred acres for glebe land.

Payback

Lieutenant Henry Waterhouse on the spearing of Governor Phillip, Manly Beach, September 1790

We should not have come, lightly armed, poorly manned.
He labours at their friendship,
sends to England for apparel,
puts a barber on the beach for their beards,
brings wine and hatchets for the feast.
Even now I hear him mutter *No revenge, no revenge.*

We came to humour Bennelong
dancing in his red kersey jacket,
besmeared in pipe clay and blood.
A whale beached a week since, putrid yet devoured.
It is old, its nose covered in barnacles,
its huge eye staring out in pity.

Not the least dress upon them,
children defecate near where they broil their meat.
None of them decent. What is life without decency?
They eat grubs, drink the blood of the goanna,
their huts the most miserable you ever saw,
no better than pigs' sties.

And they are crueller than children.
They burned a convict. Tore the skin off his back.
And they are deceitful. The one that threw the lance
picked it up with his foot. It entered the Governor,
swung in the wound like a harpoon, dragged
on the ground. *For God's sake haul it out of me.*

I broke it for him. The barbs point out his back,
fish teeth like needles, flesh hangs on them.
He bleeds and sleeps. We pull against a breeze,
Captain Collins looks upon his eye lids.
There will be promotions. I row back to the cove,
to likely opportunities.

Redemption

James Ruse at his farm, Rose Hill, Parramatta River,
December 1791

I James Ruse, now of Parramatta
ten miles up-river of the famine,
have harvested two hundred bushels from thirty acres,
have served my sentence.

The farm hand from Launceston
has fed convicts and marines alike,
ploughed out his life priced at two silver watches
at Bodmin Assizes.

I carried his Lieutenant to the shore,
grand and sparkling on my back,
I James Ruse, the first to face the land,
dreamed of Cornwall

where the grit stone tore the skin
between my fingers till my hands
bled silver, harsher than the grasses
of the Parramatta.

One day the Governor will go
and I will continue to plant and grow.
I have my eyes on the Hawkesbury River,
on horses and hogs.

We Give Thanks

Reverend Johnson decides he must build a church,
February 1793

Milbah my new child thrives. Her hands open
and close, I stroke the folds, and Araboo
the native girl, her fingers pick ripening
fruit, pulp oats and pease. Cucumbers

I have a thousand, a wheat field and even
an orchard where my boy, stillborn lies.
The drought sowed pain. Weeks of headaches,
a maddening rash, blood poured from me.

Five years here still no church, we crowd
into the boat house like conspirators.
The bible is your church, the Governor shouts,
do you suppose a house can make a carpenter?
I have acres. I shall dig up, lay out
the mud bricks myself, hew down the palm trees.
Man must have walls, an end to what he believes.

Bennelong in London

Bennelong after the death of his friend Yemmerawanne, Eltham,
May 1794

Father you stole me, tied me,
made my tongue turn like yours.

While our words mixed like colours Be-anga,
another man took my woman across the shore.

I paid you back with the spear, I had to.
Your forgiveness carried me across the black seas to here.

I have not met your King, I have met your Isabella
who has nursed me, tried to save my friend

Yemmerawanne. Alone, I made a ceremony for him.
I am invisible now, lazy as the moon.

There are men under bridges who cannot read the stars.
Some will come home on ships, some strangled where they are.

Once we were like long ago, when all
had been made, yet all was in darkness.

I shall be home when the Emu is in the sky.
Then I will leave my English clothes for good,
keep a handkerchief.

Departure

Arthur Phillip at home in the town of Bath, Somerset, July 1796

Bennelong rode with me
to Chislehurst to meet Lord Sydney.
Blue and buff striped breeches,
pepper coat, hat, buckle and shoes. My gentleman friend.

When Bennelong sang Edward Jones wrote down his songs.
We went to Sadlers Wells, St Pauls,
he listened with me to Haydn.
Handel is not for us. Was not to our taste.

We caused a stir at Covent Garden,
the two of us strolling along Mayfair.
He said of Sydney, said of his appearance:
Koolah face, like the bear.

He has written to me, asking for handkerchiefs,
stockings and shoes. Of '*muzzy doings*'
among his people while he was here,
here in my drawing room, standing straight as always.

The joy I felt on reaching Falmouth.
The waters here will flush out my malady.
Each evening people pay a shilling
to see a kangaroo at the Lyceum.

**Time
Signature**

Time Signature

Last time you were here, home that is,
there was a heartbeat. Early days
but already, there was a heartbeat.
We felt its pulse in our sleep –

your mother first, then passed
onto me, each of us picking up its refrain
softening in the heat of darkness,
playing on the roof tiles under the rain.

It walked with the birds at dawn
and the sky moved across it,
drawing light out on its count.
Louder still after you boarded the plane,
leaving us with the weekly arithmetic.

Three seasons later Rosa's fingers reach
from a photo frame. I lean in to the new-born
smell, to the film over her eyes,
get the cases down from the loft.

We're looking at clothes, maps, real estate.
Outside cloud shadows cast across fields,
where you live smoke rolls itself towards the ocean.
Here England crumbles at the edges,
twelve hours behind and counting.

The Passenger Bird

On Kangaroo Island, we have the place to ourselves.
After dark, ours the only light in the chalet park,
a lighthouse for the crepuscular caretaker.

We drive its roads for a week and find no one.
Road-kill piled at lamppost intervals
mounds of wet washing greying in the sun,

a kangaroo upright and dumbfounded at asphalt,
a koala on all fours, stoned with indecision.
Even when I see a joey move inside a pouch –

the mother broken and fly-tipped – we keep going,
tearing through the scrub of the low island
crouched like a crab in the Southern Ocean.

A shadow rolls across the road,
then a punch on the windscreen.
A blackbird slides down in front of us,

its wings splayed in a failed embrace.
All the way back the off-side wiper nudges it;
it hangs on, wing a torn flag, a pitiful hand-signal.

At night eyes muster beyond the porch.
In the morning the bird has gone.
A smear on the windscreen, cleaned by the wiper-blade.

Barely Tame

We are on the quay buying sun-cream –
pelicans and painted fish at arms-length,
day trips to see the whales – when all I can look at
is this dog of sorts, dancing in the sun.

It tugs at the harness with its teeth,
bucks at the end of its lead,
the owner, a girl, tries to calm it gingerly.
I wonder if it's the heat – the day's or its own –

sand on its back, soil on its ears,
frost settled around its neck – dingo.
Driving its tongue into an armpit, eyes in revolt,
pressing its teeth around a wrist – a cub's neck,

paws pushed against its mother's face,
fighting for its place in the pack –
creature from a guidebook, outside a gift-shop.
The girl calls out a name, it bounds,

looks into her eyes, then into the sky.
A man shouts from behind a double ice cream
You can shoot that, shoot that if you want.
It howls in mourning and licks her face.

Ten Pound Alan

Fastest runner in the school, I watched him
ease ahead of me on sports days, his chest
pressed against the finishing tape, first every time.
A good fighter, brilliant at rounders, climbing trees,
he once ate dog biscuits in my back garden,
sitting in a deck chair, Fritz's paws on his knees.

I wasn't sure what emigrating meant.
How far was that? I was afraid to ask.
I knew where he was going though.
That country in the corner of the map on the wall,
spread out like orange peel.
Ages and ages on holiday.

We went to his house before they left.
I sat on the floor by the fire pulling threads
from the carpet, a varnished boomerang
above me on the wall. His mother, poised
in front of net curtains, a silhouette inside silver
cigarette smoke, talked about the wages out there.

It was June, we stood in assembly
holding blue hymn books,
too much sun in the hall. The teacher,
her long dress yellow with flowers,
asks us all to wave to Alan. He hands me his book,
runs along the row, down the corridor,
looking back at no one.

The Fatal Shore

After Robert Hughes

She says *It is better here,*
younger and better by far.

Waves suck me in,
the pearly cockatoo tells me so,
blue mist waits over oceans
of un-surrendered land and air.

You could move here,
move away from all of that.

What would I do
but fathom the colours of the Southern Ocean
under implacable sunshine?

> *He died chained beside me*
> *before we reached the shore*

I don't want 'no worries'

> *half-mad with starvation and scurvy.*

exhausting bonhomie

> *Seven years transportation*

a torpor of contentment

> *for a pair of stockings.*

and I'd never make the journey.

> *Spewed out of London,*
> *swallowed by the passage.*

She squats to the shells, sifts one for me,
blows the sand out for a wish.
Take this back across the world.
A photo frame away her mother
stares into the terrifying perfection.

No Man's Land

Portadown, Co. Armagh 1973

My cousin sends me out to the offie,
silver shillings in my palm for coke and crisps.
Sunday, nearly night, the streets a hushed audience.
I turn from a cul-de-sac into the land of six o clock news reels,

under flags and bunting, past film set lampposts.
Eyes interpret me – my high street clothes,
the walk brought over on the boat. The voice of a boy,
brittle with grievance, shouts a question.

Outside the shop eyes weigh me up against the darkness.
Then it comes, shuffling around the corner,
brutal and discreet; an armoured vehicle.
It pauses in my path, breathing heavily.

Its lid scrapes, turns, lifts – a boy in saggy camouflage surfaces,
holds his rifle casually like luggage.
Oi mate, have you heard any gunfire round here?
I push in some crisps, tighten my lips, shake my head. *Sure?*

I swallow and confess – *Nah mate, I don't think so.*
Are you English? Oi he's English, what you doing here?
I'd dribbled balls past kids his age,
left them on the halfway line looking the wrong way.

He tells me his town, I tell him mine – we're in a park in Watford.
I might have heard shooting, from that direction, or maybe…
He descends – a voice inside the chamber – whispers by a neighbour.
It trundles off, a tank in slippers. I run back to a cul-de-sac.

Missing

Eddie, chewing a finger
resting his head against a window.
An eye fills with blood.

Takes a swig of water
sucks the zip on his jacket
sees a woman he can word up.

The skin on his fist,
tight as a stocking
craves a scab on his knuckle.

His eyes close, he hears a thud
then silence. A cry passes outside,
dragged off down the line.

Sees in the window lines on his cheek,
Eddie dives into his hood.
Eddie leans into the aisle.

Passengers opposite,
passengers a carriage away,
already alighted into nightfall,

face newspapers, their muted reflections
inside earphones, longing the sofa,
a meal on their lap.

Eddie, inside the wires
across the TV guide
streaming into living rooms

in engine time,
not speaking or blinking
picking his rhythm

dot matrix – slow – grainy – soundless Eddie,
just for the camera,
making his way towards her
missing his stop.

Confession

It's the first thing he asks you,
Did you see me on Jeremy Kyle?
Ryan, friends with everyone in prison,
sweatshirt too long in the arm
mouth too wide, face open, trod upon.
A field under rain.

I ask him what he's in here for
For cars and other daft things,
things you wouldn't like me for.

His voice rises in slow strides,
vowels bending like arrows,
an arch into a church,
words giddy with the height or the load.

His mum on the gear
while he was bobbing in and out of care,
like a queue for confession.

Ryan, next to her on the telly,
knees to his chest, ankles off the floor.
That's when I found out she was a prostitute,
and the audience were shouting her down down
which only made me love her even more.

A cloud comes to the window in the spire above.
Back in his cell *The Jeremy Kyle Show,*
the bank holiday sleep,
the celebrity touched Easter weekend.
Give him a round of applause.

The Pitch

I have worked out the weight of every jacket potato
against the price of the pitch. Passed my Food Hygiene,
whilst I've been in here.

There will be chairs beside my van. Men talking
holidays, horse races. I'll flip the breakfasts,
count out the change, toss plates into a bin.

Poached eggs like pillows,
burgers a perfume reminding men of lay-bys,
match days, weekend ice creams.

Teas – a blanket poured inside
a scaffolder gone grey with the cold,
and the weight of regret.

My uncle will bring the van then tow it home
in time for me to get to yours for tea. I can read
her a story but not stay, not unless.

I think this all through at night
as prisoners shout from their windows,
I am up there wearing an apron,
taking orders yelled out from the back of the queue.

Too Late

In the governor's office, I have no questions.
I've slept well since I got the news –
no more phone calls from custody sergeants,
people he owed money to barking at the door.

He checks his notes, *Shall we go over?*
Never ending lawns, well-kept flower beds,
two prisoners throwing grass at each other.
A pack of seagulls fighting outside the wing.

One swoops down, its beak open; I can see
its tongue. They hand me his clothes bagged and sealed.
The cell like his bedroom the day I turfed him out.
He'd leaned forward, the sheet around his neck.

A boy collecting laundry stares in on me,
edges his cart forward another door.
Beyond the window, conifers and hills,
one of those early winter sunsets, raging.

Here Lies the Giant

I regret it. Taking the money. His death.
I have buried the rest of his gold
in the pit beside him.

His death wasn't quick.
The earth rumbled like a drum,
a cloud rose when he landed,

the forest shook out its birds,
swallowed by his cries
heard across the kingdom.

People stopped, took silent,
lowered their spoons, looked to rafters.
The harp under my arm echoed his agony.

He lay there breathing, face down
steaming like a dray horse,
a newt swam in his blood.

His moaning darkened the skies,
I walked for three days
came back in the rain, he was cold.

I closed his eyes,
his lashes a brush on my fingers.
All night I dug the hole.

My mother disgusts me.
She pirouettes in her new dress,
her necklace, her harlot shoes.

And look who's back –
eggs in his pocket, arms around her waist –
does not make him my father.

There is another land, close to the sun.
The voyage is a climb, you must hold the mast
tightly through oceans of sky.

There is a house, like this one,
a widow who saved my bones,
she waits in the kitchen, stirring broth alone.

Shoots have appeared from where he lies.
In my sleep I hear them push, feel the beanstalk grow.
I will sharpen the axe, sit down with my father
one last time, fore I go.

Field

Clouds avalanche south east to north.
Gusts surf the grass – the wind deep.
I hack at ground crammed with rainfall,
each spade-full heaving a drunk to his feet.

A day's wind and it will seal itself,
become a car bonnet for the pick.
The hedge cowers looking for cover,
a rock kicks back up the shaft.

I will have to leave this field –
the waterlogged willow,
the deer cropped rowan, the minute's sun,
the hour's calm gazing at the pond

for a stroll down to the ocean
in the long mediocrity of a climate.
For a house builder to come, the carport, caravan,
someone assembling decking to Radio One.

Grass roots lie deep as bones,
my blister hardens but never heals.
A stoat leaps, rain moves off the hill –
a wedding dress blown across a field.

Pond

I dig in slow swings for four days. The hillside
breaks two shafts, snaps a fork, sends me to the surgery.
In the end the gravedigger comes,
scoops a pit big enough for a family.

I stand in it, palms on my back,
rest my head against clay under an April field.
A spider, fat as a currant teeters on an edge,
legs testing the ground above Atlantis.

After a week of puddling and sloping the sides,
I line it, fill it, my breaths slowing as water climbs
holds its nerve at the brim. Watch it for a summer, a winter,
blacken, thicken, clear, till it teems with itself.

Come spring I lie down, tap the surface like a painted wall.
I'm waiting for the newts I knew as a boy,
fetched home in tins to a basin in the garden –
I'd emptied the woodland pond of them.

Frogs call expecting rain.
A pair of crocodile eyes behind an iris.
I hold my breath, my hand crawls towards it,
then withdraws. A skater flicks to another shore.

Sky

Behind us the field's reach to horizon.
Sky charged and moving, clouds group then merge
banking north. We watch one bleed through another,
its centre deepens, the edges glow.

Some days, the evenly grey, we close the blinds.
On others we stand on chairs for the heavens'
ploughed field. Or walk to the top of the hill,
look up from the bottom of a well.

North Gower Triptych

I   Saltmarsh

On a half-land weeping to sea
between beach and berries,

sunken horses, bellies dropped
to brooklets, noses mud scarred,

comb the shorn grass.
Dusty sloes, papery sea holly

line the ends of the marsh.
The ground hardens.

September. Looking both ways,
trusting the sun to hold its ground.

The pines are bare to their elbows.
In the distance nothing but the wide light.

II   *Beach*

Over the ramparts of the dunes
sea shrinking back to mean low water.

We are at the bay's lip, the fly tip of the river,
heading west on our walk's middle stretch.

Faces down to the drift wood,
Norwegian litter, waves out of sort with the shore.

The loud-mouthed wind
splits us like a child scheming.

I look up and you are no longer there,
drop down scoop up a shell, I will put in a drawer,

catch up at the headland. We rest before
the last climb to the squat bell-tower.

III Church

The porch dips before the door,
the temperature slips inside.

An information sheet, folded three ways,
a visitors' book beginning to curl, water drips from the tower.

At the back – kettle, cups and vestments.
A bible is open, the place is swept.

The solitary plaque, our fingers along the font's lip.
Velvet dresses the plate, milk sticks to the carton.

Always we walk the aisle but never sit,
conscious of what others might think.

The half sunken headstones.
The graveyard that slopes to the road.

Seeds

Pulled apart berries, flower-head flakes,
the toffee coloured discs inside iris pods.
Everything from beads down to dots, snipped,
crumbled into a handmade chocolate box.

They are resting. Kindling on an unlit fire.
The smell of a damp shed comes from them.
The smell of spring's stem. Until the moisture
goes the way of August leaving merely chemistry.

It might be years before they fatten the hedge.
Some will never burst. Some flecks on my finger
I will cup in my palm as poppies, remembering the splinter
my mother dug from my hand, ribbons bleeding into water.

South Gower Triptych

I   Holloway

Hole-ways hide down low between churches.
They start and end here that we might look up.

We move at root level. Unseen, under-field,
unnoticed by cattle, udders at head height.

This is worn ground. From *holweg* to *holewaye,*
presence of a passage way, Iron Age traffic.

Cart after horse, after goats, after a hawk on a glove
after wolves, all before the walks for Whitsun-ale.

A tree arches into the moss zone. Light squints
off water spilling down the gutter of the gulley.

We are quietened, slowed, until the hedge spins ahead,
widened at its fern funnel, pipe rising to down.

II   Down

The heath is a knee deep wade. It's left alone, almost.
Dogs run out the nightjars, ponies chew tussocks,

but it's treacherous enough to save itself –
the asphodel flower, reddening now, poisons the sheep.

We have the company of remains. A levelled radar station,
standing stones and a burial chamber.

Gorse-light dazzles mid-afternoon, spikes
around the pillaged rubble of a ruin.

Each time we come here, something else has been laid down,
poured onto the ground. We all carry the teem.

On the cusp of the bay I watch a car move into a new space,
over the sea a Heinkel comes in low, level out of the sun.

III   Sea

I longed for the sea all day. When it came
at the down's end it blended with the sky.

I go in against the wind, the shingle, your cold advice,
swim out far enough to see you smalled at the arc of the bay.

The beach bobs above my head, now sky darker than water.
Colder gusts of a rip tide rush about my ankles.

Rain slips into mist, the surface simmers across a distance,
you are downstage wheeling me in but I stay.

It's the only sea we have and I won't give it up – the reward
of this trauma – not for both towels or some other painted ocean.

It comes down my nose for the rest of the day, stiffens my skin.
I leave its dust in my hair until the end of the week.

Leaves

They come in a rush like children out of school.
The willow sprinting, the birch behind,
bright-lined creases looking up to the light –
an infant's hand unfolded in mine last year.

Between my fingers a blackcurrant leaf –
a colander full, air thick with wine in my mother's kitchen.
Come Christmas I'll heap dead leaves to feed the buds,
my finger in Rosa's palm, *round and round the garden.*

Waiting for Bats

The sun crawls off, churning up evening.
Mosquitoes swim in the dimness.
They come from their coma –
mammal-kites, beetle-birds, twitching
out of cold stone. We stand and count them
as they scale the gusts, pitch themselves
at ricochets, turn us, stoop us.
One trails another in a frenzy of pairing
or rage. I cast up a pebble to break a wave,
a bat spins back, flies headfirst towards the joke
every time.

They are alive again. They have survived
the renovation of ruins,
the coldblooded walls of winter.
They go on living in dark
while we wait at the edges of light
for shorter days. We can go inside
close the blind, lie down together.

Mid Wales Triptych

I   Afon Arban

Five miles of sinking, prodding, pools and ruts, sodden
along the river, between the dam and the forest.

Sheep group on scraps of green, some trees
climb from gullies, heads above the skyline.

Bog and hummock, grass growing into straw,
the moorland empties us into silence.

The forest comes in a black line, burying the river.
It is breezeless, clouds of powdered pine, our eyes

wear tinted lenses, we break branches, follow the snap
down plantation aisles to a track,

hard core underfoot for three miles. Sunlight.
We slide down, deep in moss to hazel, oak and Afon Tywi.

II   *Bunkhouse*

Squat and white, half buried on the valley floor.
Just us and the warden, dried pasta, gas,

the crippled solar lighting, signs on every cupboard door,
above the sink, stories of redundancy and divorce.

We wait on a slate floor for drinking water to boil,
scent of semolina, someone sneaking lager into a dorm.

The warden runs his thumb across a map
points to farmers slashing tyres,

letting dogs loose in yards. We drink by a garden bench
keeping a swallow from her nest.

I arch my back unfolding fingers of a fern,
downstream the valley pours away to a bridge.

III   Doethie Valley

Spur behind spur, hands clasped in prayer.
We weave around curves until the land unfolds

to a floodplain of two pleading palms.
Fern ravaged ruin, wild orchid, high grass

ready to spawn, seed-heads on our hands.
We can walk no more then walk for miles. Camp,

moulding ourselves over contours of earth,
twisting in sacks, sliding down ground

that looked flat, shuffling back, elbows clenched
through wind-slapping darkness.

Water dribbles down from the tent's skin,
until we give up, crawl out again.

Llanmadoc Hill

It looks as easy as an apple.
Fairy tale round, ferns reddening,
ripe for the taking.

I switch off the news channel,
we head for a gap in the gorse,
take on the plump slope in short steps,

crumbling rust, scattering spores.
We look down at the haze over Rhossili,
the steam from a pony's muzzle,

breath in the beginnings of Autumn.
Our legs straighten at the iron-age fort,
the hill-top a rug rolled up into ramparts.

We can see the beach, the estuary,
know the election result will be in by now.
Behind the sand a wall has been breached,
land is sea-washed, bleached to marsh.

Hill of Faith

John Wesley in Heptonstall, May 1747

We ascend over the shadow of crows, stooped
like goats on the hill. Weavers lock their doors
on callers, their heads bowed to the loom,
hands tied to the wool, minds to the cloth hall,

the tavern. Where is the light on the stony tops?
Up here the word of God is blown about
to moorland tussocks, the broken rocks,
women's faces cracked by storms, mouths

crying hymns that carry to the lee side
of the hill and further up to Slack;
one gave me rose-syrup when I was dry.
We will a chapel build when I come back,
with eight strong sides, a door never locked
so the wind will turn away, but never the flock.

Folly

All summer they rebuilt the shopping centre.
Layer upon layer of grey,
yellow hats and jackets sinking behind blocks,
the crane poised like a spout.
Men were relentless.
Their drills cut through our phone calls,
my whispers at your desk.

Their blue torches flamed into our sunsets
as I waited for people to leave, to log out, lock draws, *just go*
to free me to walk to your chair,
and as the last rivet rang out
I'd turn you round and we'd kiss the town quiet.

Do you remember when the floor collapsed?
A man yelled in torment,
Get me out of here!
girders at thirty degrees ringing like bells.
People below stopped or ran
but I held onto you,
hooked my hands on the warmth beneath your cardigan.

Why weren't we somewhere else?
There was the park, the meadows,
once or twice my little house,
with your car parked two streets away.
When winter came you said we'd gone as far as we could.
I thought of hands burning on scaffolding.
Saw the frost harden on fresh concrete.

Reckoning

Padraig Pearse, Good Friday 1916

My letters are written, debts acknowledged,
some verses unfinished. I took communion
this evening, settled my disputes with God.
There remains one last play, one stark, true action.

My uniform is too tight in the trousers,
a little loose in the shoulders. My sword,
my revolver. History is a shroud
I offer to share at Liberty Hall

from under a portrait of Tone. War is loved
by people; the boy at the barricade,
his mother at the grave. Birth comes with blood.
A century has passed since last it was staged.
The fallen, the risen body of Christ
reminds us what our tongues are for at last.

The Last Room

He takes the hair oil from the cabinet,
the razor, the long serving aftershave,
wipes the sandwich-board face he has worn
across forty years of the shop floor.

He turns both shoulders
buttons the blazer, his back a lawn of blue,
bordered by a chequered cravat
an ocean away from the sailing shoes.

Cleans out his pipe, walks out
searching for a garden rich with roses,
the low race of house martins, a piano,
someone half-singing Vera Lynn.

For a pier bombed into the sea,
the Capstan cigarette lit hours
behind khaki doors, for the laughter
as he carried her case into the room.

In the pub on the promenade she smiled
leg swinging from the bar stool.
Those sudden years before the kids came,
drinking, dancing in Streatham ballroom.

Beside her now in the dayroom
she remembers a song,
the nurse breaks her round to listen.
He talks to her above the television, always on.

He finds himself between the co-op
and the kitchen, flexing his newspaper,
clearing his throat, swallowing
his disappointment with the government.

The post comes, he reads a newsletter
for retired union members.
The microwave blinks, he squints at the numbers,
takes a treat down to the home each afternoon.

Notes and Acknowledgments

Thanks are due to the editors of the following publications, where early versions of some of these poems were first published – *Acumen, Clear Poetry, Envoi, The Interpreters House, Prole Journal, The High Window* and *Back Room Poets.* Some appeared in *Close to Home* (Prole Books). *Too Late* won first prize in Back Room Poets International Poetry competition 2015, *Confession* won the Prole Laureate competition in 2014. *First Fleet* received time to write support from Arts Council England and I would particularly like to thank my mentor, poet Sarah Corbett. Sarah's guidance, editorial support and encouragement have helped the development and completion of this collection, as well as my progress in the ongoing voyage to become a poet.

In researching the first sequence I read a lot of primary and secondary sources. I began with Robert Hughes's magnificent 1987 history, *The Fatal Shore* and Tom Keneally's beautifully vivid *The Commonwealth of Thieves.* I then moved on to the journals of Arthur Phillip, Watkin Tench, Surgeon White and others. I would like to thank the Clements Library, University of Michigan, for kind permission to quote the words of Jacob Nagle from *The Nagle Journal,* italicised in the poem *Mercy.*

Two images used for the front cover are reproduced by kind permission of the State Library of New South Wales. *Jacob Nagle his Book A.D. One Thousand Eight Hundred and Twenty Nine May 19th. Canton. Stark County Ohio, 1775-1802,* compiled 1829 (digital order no. a366103). *Tracks of the Sirius & Waakzaamheydt in the Southern Hemisphere, 1787-1792* by William Bradley. Charts from his journal: *A Voyage to New South Wales1802* (digital order no. a138492).

Arabanno was abducted by marines on New Year's Eve 1788 in an attempt to learn more about the land they were colonising and the language of the indigenous peoples. Initially restrained he lived freely amongst the settlers until his death from smallpox six months later. Surgeon White records that Arabanno referred to the disease as *galgalla*.

Bennelong was captured in November 1789. He escaped from the settlement after six months but then renewed his contact with the Governor. In 1790 Bennelong asked the Governor to build him a hut on what became known as Bennelong Point, where Sydney Opera House now stands. He learned English and travelled with Phillip to England in 1792 living with Henry Waterhouse. He returned to Sydney Cove in 1795.

Thomas Barrett had a previous death sentence commuted before a second saw him transported to New South Wales. En route he fashioned belt buckles into fake quarter dollars whilst below deck. Impressed by his ability Surgeon White gave him a silver kidney dish to engrave. Now in the National Museum of Australia, the Charlotte Medal is said to be the first work of Australian colonial art. Aged about eighteen, Barrett was convicted of theft of food from the stores and became the first person to be hanged in the colony.

Samuel Bird escaped from the colony in 1791, and with eight others eventually arrived in Timor where he was recaptured by naval officers in search of the *Bounty* mutineers. He died on the voyage home to England.

Catherine Crowley became the mistress of aristocrat convict D'Arcy Wentworth during the journey of the Second Fleet. Her son, William, with the in-turned eye, was with two other settlers, among the first white Australians to cross the Blue Mountains. He became a prominent poet, journalist and politician and a principal advocate of the name 'Australia.'

James Daley claimed to have found a gold mine up river from the settlement and was flogged for his deception. He was hanged at the end of 1788 for stealing from another's tent.

Jane Fitzgerald lived with William Mitchell, a private in the marines. She was sentenced to twenty five lashes for disobedience. Little else is known.

John Hudson at aged eleven was the youngest male convict on the First Fleet. He was sent to Norfolk Island in 1790 and received fifty lashes in 1791 for being outside his hut after hours.

Reverend Richard Johnson and his wife had a daughter who was given the Aboriginal name Milbah. They also adopted an Aboriginal child orphaned by smallpox. In 1793 tired of the Governor's refusals, he began to build a church himself.

Jacob Nagle was an American seaman of the First Fleet who sailed with the *Sirius* during its remarkable voyage to purchase supplies from Cape Town at the end of 1788.

Governor Arthur Phillip was fifty years old in 1788 and a highly experienced naval officer. He was seen at the time in England and in the colony, as possessing too lenient an attitude towards the convicts and an over friendly approach to Aboriginal people.

James Ruse was a Cornish farmhand sentenced to seven years transportation. After a year he produced the first successful wheat harvest in the colony. There is now a James Ruse Agricultural College.

Watkin Tench was a young captain whose two journals about the voyage and settlement are among the most celebrated. They remain widely read today.

Surgeon White wrote an illustrated journal. Though he had some skill as an artist it is believed many of the drawings were by the convict Thomas Watling

Henry Waterhouse was a marine officer present at the spearing of Phillip. He is commemorated in the name of Waterhouse Island north east of Tasmania.